How to Write a Successful Book Proposal In 8 Days or Less

By
Patricia L. Fry

Matilija Press
PMB 123
323 E. Matilija St., Ste 110
Ojai, CA 93023

How to Write a Successful Book Proposal In 8 Days or Less

Matilija Press
PMB 123
323 E. Matilija St., Ste. 110
Ojai, CA 93023
www.matilijapress.com
plfry620@yahoo.com

Second Edition, Revised
Copyright © by Patricia L. Fry
ISBN 0-9612642-9-2

First Edition published as an ebook in 2004

All rights reserved
Printed in the United States of America

TABLE OF CONTENTS

How to Write a Successful Book Proposal In 8 Days or Less

Introduction iv

Class #1: What is a Book Proposal? 1
Sample Query Letter 11
Sample Cover Letter 13

Class #2: The Synopsis 15
Sample Synopsis 18

Class #3: The Synopsis Continued 22

Class #4: Your Marketing Strategies 25
Book Signing Tips for Authors 31
Sample of Marketing Strategies 37

Class #5: Market Analysis/Competitive Works 39
Sample of Market Analysis 41

Class #6: About the Author 44
Sample of About the Author 46

Class #7: Chapter Outline 50
Sample of a Chapter Outline 54

Class #8: Putting it All Together 58

Index 65

How to Write a Successful Book Proposal
In 8 Days or Less

During the summer of 2004, I taught an online book proposal class through Writing-World.com. During this eight-week course, students who studied the lectures and completed the assignments each produced a potentially successful book proposal. In fact, one of them landed a publishing contract with a major publishing house. I'm now offering this course in book form for those of you who wish to work at your own pace. With this guide, you can create a book proposal—from title page to completed Chapter Outline—in eight days or less. I know this is possible, because I've successfully tested it out. I completed the proposal for my book, *The Right Way to Write, Publish and Sell Your Book* in exactly one week.

Who is Patricia Fry? I've been writing for publication for over thirty years, having contributed hundreds of articles to about 190 different magazines. I also have twenty-two books to my credit, most of which originated from a book proposal. I work with clients on their successful book proposals. And I've written numerous articles and book chapters on this topic.

Here is your complete guide to producing a successful book proposal. For additional guidance, please contact me. While I will volunteer an opinion or a suggestion here and there, I do charge for larger blocks of my time and for more generous portions of my expertise. My professional fees are posted at www.matilijapress.com/consulting.html

By Patricia L Fry
Plfry620@yahoo.com
http://www.matilijapress.com

Book Proposal Class

1

WHAT IS A BOOK PROPOSAL?

A book proposal is a sales pitch—a business plan for your book. I strongly urge hopeful authors to write a book proposal BEFORE starting their book. Most publishers and agents, once you've attracted their attention with your incredible query letter, will request a book proposal. Some publishers (and agents) have specific requirements for a book proposal, but don't let that throw you. Once you've developed a book proposal using the basic guidelines presented here, you can easily tweak it to meet any special requirements.

The first step to winning a publisher's (or agent's) heart and soul is to write a spectacular query letter. Why write a query letter when you have a perfectly good book proposal? The answer is simple—because the publisher will probably request it. Publishers and agents often receive hundreds of submissions each month. That many query letters received are easier to manage than the same number of completed manuscripts or proposals. Most publishers, today, prefer an introduction to your project through a one-to two-page query letter. Publishers sometimes change their specialty or they are inundated with certain topics or genres. You will save everyone time by sending a query letter as a first step.

Some publishers and agents prefer receiving the completed manuscript or a book proposal, first. Always obtain a copy of the publisher's/ agent's Submission Guidelines or Guidelines for Authors and comply with their particular submission requirements.

AUTHOR'S GUIDELINES

Often, you'll find Author's Guidelines or Guidelines for Authors or Submission Guidelines on a publisher's Web site. I worked with a client today who said she was having trouble finding Submission Guidelines on publisher Web sites. Some publishers do make it difficult. If you don't see a link to their Guidelines on the home page, go to their *About Us* page or their *Contact* page. Sometimes you will find the information you seek on the *Editorial* page. If you can't locate the Guidelines on any of these pages, email a request for a copy. Or you can request a copy by mail. Be sure to enclose an SASE (self-addressed-stamped envelope). To get an idea about the type of manuscripts a publisher wants and his basic submission requirements, study this publishing company's listing in *Writer's Market, Literary Market Place* or other similar reference books. But always request Submission Guidelines from those publishers to whom you want to submit your manuscript.

Why are Submission Guidelines so important? Let me count the ways. Publishers, these days specialize. A publisher is not a one-size-fits-all proposition anymore. While some publishers have several specialties, others specialize just in health books, text books, history, cooking or children's books, for example. It is important, in today's highly competitive publishing climate, that you choose the right publisher for your project.

One way to make sure that you're submitting to an appropriate publisher is to study his Guidelines for Authors. His catalog of books is important, too, unless he has recently changed his specialty.

I often speak with publishers who are no longer pursuing their signature line of cookbooks or true crime books, for example, and are now soliciting arts and craft books or detective novels. You'll want to know this before you waste your time submitting your great idea to the wrong publisher.

Some publishers are pretty specific about what is in the proposal you send. While some are primarily interested in just the synopsis and the marketing section, others might want a condensed (two or three-page) version of your entire proposal. A few publishers will dictate exactly how many books they'd like you to include in your Market Analysis section and the number of pages or words your synopsis should comprise.

NONFICTON BOOK PROPOSAL

A nonfiction book proposal consists of a Cover Letter, Title Page, Synopsis (or Overview), Enhancements Page (optional), Marketing Section/Promotional Ideas (who is your audience, how do you suggest this book be promoted and what will you do to promote it?), Market Analysis or Comparison of Competitive Works, About the Author, Chapter Outline and an SASE (self-addressed-stamped envelope). Most publishers also want to see a few sample chapters. Some request the first chapter and two others which you feel are good representations of your project. Other publishers might want to see the first fifty pages of your book.

BOOK PROPOSAL FOR A NOVEL

A fiction book proposal might include a Cover Letter, Synopsis, About the Author and an SASE. I suggest including your promotional ideas in your cover letter. Some publishers of fiction aren't interested in seeing a book proposal. They just want you to send the manuscript. But there are reasons for writing a book proposal other than just pleasing a publisher.

WHY WRITE A BOOK PROPOSAL?

Of course, one reason for writing a book proposal is because the publisher has requested it. A good book proposal can sell a book. But the most important reason is for you. You wouldn't start a business without a business plan. Well, remove those rose-colored glasses because it's time you understand that publishing is a business. Enter this field with any other mindset and you will fail—thousands of people, each year, do.

Think of writing as art, if you wish. But once you decide to publish what you write, you are shifting from creative to business mode. You must switch off your right brain and engage the left. Your book, then,

3

becomes a product and a book proposal is a business plan for that product.

You can learn volumes by writing a book proposal. You'll find out whether you have a book at all. For example, if you can't write a synopsis or come up with a chapter outline, you probably don't have a handle on your book idea, yet. It would not make good business sense to pursue this project, would it?

The process of writing a book proposal will help you discover whether you have an audience for your book. Is there a market for books of this type? What you learn through the process of writing a book proposal may, in fact, cause you to change your focus. For example, you may have your heart set on producing a book describing various WWII aircraft. Your research might indicate, however, that there's more need and interest in the stories behind the assembly and testing of these planes.

A book proposal is a guide for writing the book. Once you've written a complete book proposal, writing the book is practically a slam dunk. Think about it, you've fleshed out the theme of your book—you are clear about the subject matter and you have a chapter outline—you are ready to write a book.

I meet a lot of authors who give little thought to their audience until AFTER they write their book. They have a book in them and they just want to get it out. And that's okay. It's when they decide that they also want their book to become a bestseller that they run into problems. These authors experience disappointment after disappointment and it's primarily because they did not bother to write a *business plan* for their book. They did not consider their audience or the market. They wrote their book strictly to massage their ego.

I have to admit that, in the early years of my career, I balked at the idea of writing a book proposal. I didn't want to be bothered. I just wanted to write. Now, whether I plan to find a publisher for my book or self-publish, I always write a book proposal first and I highly recommend that you do, too.

A book proposal is a guide for writing the book. Once you've written a complete book proposal, writing the book is practically a slam dunk. Think about it, you've fleshed out the theme of your book—you are clear about the subject matter and you have a chapter outline—you are ready to write the book.

A WORD ABOUT POD

Unfortunately, the new breed of fee-based POD publisher doesn't care about seeing a book proposal. They don't scrutinize the manuscripts they receive. They just accept large sums of money from hopeful authors and go ahead and publish their, often, inferior books.

As far as I'm concerned, it's okay to pay a POD publisher to produce your book, as long as you make it your business to become well informed about the publishing industry and about such services BEFORE signing on the dotted line. And part of this education is to write a book proposal.

> A fee-based POD publisher is different than a POD printer. The POD publisher produces your book for a fee of anywhere from $99 to thousands of dollars. They will provide the International Standard Book Number (ISBN), bar code, etc. They are your publisher. A POD (Print on Demand) printer simply prints your book using digital technology. I often hire a POD printing comany to print my self-published books.

The POD publisher might advertise that he can help you self-publish your book. This claim can be misleading to an inexperienced author. Self-publishing means that **you** set up a publishing company. **You** purchase your own ISBN block. **You** hire a printing company. **You** arrange and pay for every aspect of producing your book. **You** are the publisher and you reap all of the profits. When you work with a fee-based POD publisher, you are not in control and your profit is not as great. You will still be required to promote your own book, however.

A fee-based POD publisher might say that he is a royalty publisher. This can also be confusing to a hopeful author. Sure, he might pay royalties, but that's after you've paid him to produce your book. A traditional royalty publisher does not charge you (the author) to publish your book. He takes the financial risk and pays you royalties on books as they sell.

> Not all fee-based POD publishers are the same. At last count, there were over seventy-five such services in the U.S.—each with a little different program, fee structure and contract.

COVER LETTER

The Cover Letter identifies your package as a book proposal. Type it on your letterhead—be sure to include the date. If you don't have letterhead, type your name, address, phone number, email address and Web site address centered at the top of the page. Next:

1: State that this is a book proposal for (TITLE OF YOUR BOOK). I like to make the title of the book and the subtitle stand out. Type it in bold or a print size larger, for example. And be sure to use italics. Remind the publisher that he or she requested the book proposal.

2: Succinctly describe your book in one or two paragraphs. Remember that your proposal is enclosed, so this needn't be as detailed as a query letter might be. Consider borrowing a paragraph from your query letter and insert it into your Cover Letter as a way to appropriately introduce your book.

3: Give a projected delivery date for the manuscript. If the book is finished, say so. If not, offer a reasonable completion date. Once a publisher asks to see your manuscript, you will probably become highly motivated to sit down and finish it. I generally allow myself three or four months to write a book from a proposal. It's amazing what you can accomplish under fire, however. I once completed an entire sixteen-chapter book in five weeks. Remember, you already have your chapter outline which means that you've done quite a bit of research and your book is organized. It's just a matter of establishing a writing routine.

A publisher might offer you an advance of anywhere from $500 to $5000 to write the book. This should motivate you to start writing. If there is no advance and you have limited time to write, you might negotiate with the publisher. Say, for example, that you'll send the first third of the book within two or three months.

> The average length of time it takes to write a book is between three and four months or thirteen to fourteen forty-hour weeks.

4: At the end of your Cover Letter, type, "Sincerely," and your name. Under that, list the enclosures (each part of the book proposal).

> Many of you haven't noticed that the old school has changed. It is now one space after a period, colon, question mark or any other punctuation. I recommend that you use twelve-point Times New Roman for letters and manuscripts. Letters should be single-spaced with one to one and a half inch margins.

TITLE PAGE

Design a Title Page similar to a title page in a published book. Type your book title and subtitle in large letters about one-third of the way down the page. In smaller letters under that, write "by" and your name. Include your projected word count for the entire book at the bottom of the page. Look at the publisher's Guidelines for Authors to determine the size book this publisher prefers. If you can, stay within these parameters. If you can't, you may have to find a publisher who publishes books in that size range. It's okay to plug this figure in after you have completed your book proposal and have a better idea about the word count. Or just print a figure within the range this publisher requires and make sure that you stick to it when you write the book.

Many publishers today are pretty flexible as to the word count—indicating 50,000-150,000 or 40,000-80,000. Keep in mind, however, that few publishers will work with a first time author who has written an enormous tome.

> I estimate my word count after completing my book proposal. For example, if I plan to write an introduction and twelve chapters, I figure that the introduction will be approximately three pages and the chapters will encompass probably ten to fifteen pages each. If you figure 250 words per page (double-spaced), that's approximately 40,000 words. If you are targeting a publisher who wants 60,000 words, go to work expanding your ideas, thus your chapters.

I met a man at a book festival recently who asked for help in finding a publisher for his book. He told me that he, in fact, had a publisher interested but that the publisher wanted him to cut his book by half. He said that the publisher (and this is true of many publishers today) did not want to invest in such a large project with a first-time, unproven author. I suggested the obvious—"cut your manuscript down." But the man said, "I can't possibly do that. Now, what can I do to find a publisher?" Self-publishing or publishing through AuthorHouse, IUniverse or another fee-based POD publisher is probably the answer for this man and others like him who are too attached to their words to work successfully with an experienced traditional royalty publisher.

ABOUT YOUR TITLE
A title is extremely important, so take your time in choosing one. A title for a nonfiction book should be succinct. Someone who is looking for a book on this topic should be able to locate it easily. **Poor** titles for a book of dog grooming tips for the novice might be, *Beautify Your Neighborhood One Dog at a Time* or *From Ears to Paws.* These titles might not be too bad if they had succinct subtitles. For example, *Dog Grooming Tips for the Novice.*

One of my worst book titles is *Quest For Truth.* It doesn't say anything about the book, does it? And this book doesn't sell very well, either, even though, when people read it, they are absolutely fascinated. A better title for this book might be, *True Past Life Experiences* or *Adventures in Reincarnation.*

One of my best selling books is, *The Mainland Luau, How to Capture the Flavor of Hawaii in Your Own Backyard.* The title is a bit long, but people know what they are buying. Another title that has worked well for me is, *The Ojai Valley, An Illustrated History*. Someone wanting to know more about the Ojai Valley will quickly choose this book over a book called, *The Enchanted Land* or *Pink Moment Over the Topa Topa Mountains*, for example. My book, *Youth Mentoring, Sharing Your Gifts With the Future*, is pretty self-explanatory. The publisher used the title, *Write On!* for my journal-keeping book, which isn't very clear. But the subtitle, *Journal-keeping For Teens* does a pretty good job of explaining the subject of the book.

The opposite is true of novels, books of poetry and children's story books. For fiction, think *intrigue*. Be creative and clever. I headed a publishing workshop for a group of homeschool kids a few years ago. At the end of the eight-weeks, they had a published book of their works to show off. They chose the title, *Tuesday Afternoons* because that was the day of the week when we met. Their subtitle is, *Creative Writing by Ojai Valley Homeschoolers*. I once edited a book of poetry. We decided to call it, *Electric Rain*, after one of the poems in the collection. The subtitle said simply, *Poems*. Edward Yeomans, Jr. wrote a book about his father's life and named it, *Nourishing the Spirit*. This is a lovely title, but it certainly didn't give a clue as to the content of the book. But his subtitle told the story—*The Life and Views of Edward Yeomans Sr.*

Before settling on a title, study the titles for some of the books on the bestseller list and those in your genre that are popular. Look at how titles appear on the book cover—a short title might stand out more because it can be set in larger type. Consider whether you will use a significant photograph or drawing on the cover—how will your choice of titles fit in with this design? And do keep your audience in mind when considering a title. Make it easy for them to choose your book!

The bad news is that if you land a publisher, you can wave *bye bye* to your perfect title. Publishers almost always change the title when they sign a publishing contract. Maybe it's a power trip—a control thing. Or maybe they really do know what sort of titles click with people and which ones fall flat.

If you decide to self-publish your book, however, your title is strictly up to you.

TABLE OF CONTENTS
You'll also need to prepare a Table of Contents (TOC) page for your Book Proposal. The TOC comes after the Title Page, but you won't be able to complete it until you've finished your Book Proposal. For now, just follow the TOC model for this book (the one you're reading). Type "Table of Contents" at the top of the page. Under that, type "Book Proposal." List the parts of the Book Proposal: Synopsis, The Market for This Book, Promotional Ideas, Market Analysis (or Competition), About the Author, Chapter Outline and Sample Chapters. Leave space for page numbers and plug them in when they are set.

ASSIGNMENT
1: If you haven't already, come up with a title for your book. Keep in mind that you might want an intriguing, interesting title for a novel or book of poetry. Choose a catchy title for a fun, how-to book or a story book. Come up with a succinct, descriptive title for a more serious work such as a biography, history or self-help book. And just have fun with a title for a children's story book.

2: Find a publisher or two who accepts books such as the one you have in mind. I suggest that you do this now so that you will have specific guidelines to focus on while preparing your proposal.

To find an appropriate publisher, go to a bookstore or research books on Amazon.com and locate those similar to the one you are writing. Who published these books? Request their Author's Guidelines and study them carefully. Also study their catalog to make sure that your project is compatible with their book list. You can use *Writer's Market* or *Literary Market Place* (both available in the reference section of your library for free and online for a fee). Or purchase a hard copy of *Writer's Market* for around $30 at a bookstore near you. Note: the new edition of *Writer's Market* comes out each September. For example, the 2006 edition is available in September of 2005.

10

> Most hopeful authors target the major publishers first and there's nothing wrong with that as long as your project has bestselling potential. Now be realistic. A book on how to make a living walking dogs is NOT going to appeal to the masses and it will not appeal to Simon and Schuster. But there are about 300 small to medium-size traditional royalty publishers who might be interested in a book on this topic. Launch a serious study of appropriate publishers and you have a MUCH better chance of being published.

3: Write your Cover Letter, Title Page and Table of Contents.

RECOMMENDED READING
In case you want to do additional reading, here are two of my favorite books related to book proposals:

Write the Perfect Book Proposal by Jeff Herman and Deborah M. Adams is in most bookstores and available at Amazon.com. I refer to this book often because it features ten actual proposals that sold and why.

The Successful Writer's Handbook, by Patricia Fry is available through matilijapress.com, Amazon.com or can be ordered through any bookstore. This book also features other practical tools, creative ideas, useful techniques and valuable resources for freelance writers, authors and publishers.

SAMPLE QUERY LETTER
Today's Date

Publisher Name
Publishing Company
Address
City, State, Zip

Dear Ms. (or Mr.) Name:

Approximately 81 percent of the population believes they have a book in them. And many more people than ever before are actually writing their personal stories, novels and books *promoting a cause or a profession. And what's to stop them? Technology is certainly in their favor. Anyone who can type can produce a manuscript. With self-publishing so convenient and inexpensive, the opportunities for wannabe authors are boundless. Most new authors fail, however, because they go about the process of producing a book **all wrong**.*

I'd like to propose an 80,000-word book: *The Right Way to Write, Publish and Sell Your Book (or A Guide to Successful Authorship)*

There are four primary reasons why first-time authors fail. 1.) Most newbie authors write the book as a first step. 2.) They don't understand the basics of writing, marketing and promoting a book 3.) They are ignorant about the publishing industry in general. 4.) They have unreasonable expectations.

Few authors consider whether there is a market for their book. They don't know who their target audience is, how to locate and choose an appropriate publisher or even how to properly and professionally approach him/her. Too many hopeful authors blindly sign contracts with fee-based POD book producers and live to regret it. And few authors understand their responsibility in promoting their book.

In my proposed book, I suggest studying the publishing industry as a first step. A hopeful author needs to become familiar with the market and his competition. I advise first-time authors to determine their target audience and potential publishers early on. I recommend that writers build promotion into their book as they write it. I'm adamant about writing a book proposal and I guide hopeful authors through the process. Authors who follow the guide outlined in my book will experience greater intimacy with their project and experience greater success.

I devote an entire chapter to fee-based POD publishers with an emphasis on author beware. This book also includes chapters on how to organize your book, writing tips and techniques, how to work with publishers and agents, the self-publishing process, book promotion and bookkeeping tips for authors.

I've been writing for publication for over 25 years. I write articles for magazines such as Writer's Digest, Authorship, Canadian Author, Cat Fancy, Entrepreneur, Woman's Own, Kiwanis and many others. I'm the author of 22 published books and I've contributed to about half dozen other books as an expert in the publishing field. I also work with clients on their writing projects. I travel throughout the country as a speaker. Last year, I spoke at the *Much Ado About Books* event in Jacksonville, FL; the National Association of Women Writer's Conference in Arlington, TX; the SLO Book Festival in San Luis Obispo, CA and the Meet Me in St. Louis Writer's Workshop and Book Festival in MO. I had to cancel speaking engagements for Toastmasters International in Reno and for the Society of Professional Journalists in New York because I was on crutches all summer.

I have worked with traditional publishers, I've self-published, I've published through co-publishing companies and I've produced ebooks.

I'm the president of SPAWN (Small Publishers, Artists and Writers Network), a 9-year-old networking organization. I respond to member and subscriber questions regularly, often helping first-time authors through the industry maze. I also answered questions for the National Association of Women Writers members for several years.

Let me know if you'd like to see my book proposal.

Sincerely,

Patricia L. Fry
www.matilijapress.com (for more about me)
enclosures: published clips

SAMPLE COVER LETTER
Today's Date

Publisher's (or Acquisitions Editor's) Name
Publishing Company
Address
City/State/Zip

Dear Ms. (or Mr.) Name:

Per your request, I've enclosed my book proposal for *Catscapades, Tales of Ordinary and Extraordinary Cats.*

As you may recall, this is a collection of true cat stories designed to entertain, teach, fascinate, enchant, surprise and delight readers who appreciate the feline persuasion.

I'll share the story of Max, the once feral kitten who is now the purrrrfect lap cat. I'll reminisce about saving Maggie's kittens from certain death by using an on-hands healing technique. And I'll talk about using *mind talk* to coax a reluctant calico into the cat carrier. You'll meetPomPoman unusually trusting mother cat and Tina, a spayed female cat who left home and returned a year later with a newborn kitten in tow. Ialso share a story about Smoky, a Maine coon cat, and his owner's valiant attempt to save his broken tail. There are a total of 60 stories in all, including one about that fateful day when I inherited four adult cats and how their future health and happiness was secured seemingly through divine intervention.

Please review the proposal and let me know if you would like to see the entire book. I could conceivably deliver the completed manuscript to you by September 1.

Sincerely,

Patricia L. Fry
Enclosure: Book Proposal
Synopsis
Promotional Plan
Market Analysis (Competition)
About the Author
Chapter Outline
Sample Chapters

Book Proposal Class

2

THE SYNOPSIS

Today, I'm asking you to write a Synopsis or Overview of your project. The Synopsis is the meat of your book proposal. This is where you describe your story or the theme, purpose and/or point of your book. I tell would-be authors that if you can't write a one or two-page synopsis, you'd better rethink your book idea. Some experts suggest that the Synopsis be more like ten to fifteen pages. But I (and many others) agree that it should be kept to two pages single-spaced.

A Book Proposal Synopsis is in essay form. It should be organized and logical. Just as you would a story, write your Synopsis with a beginning, middle and end. You'll want to include these key points:

- What kind of book is this?
- What is your book about?
- What story does your book tell?
- What is the focus and scope of your book?
- Who is your audience?
- Why did you decide to write this book?
- What tone will you use throughout the book?
- Why do you think people will be interested in this book?
- What makes your book different, interesting or worthwhile?

Some of these points will be enhanced in other areas of the book proposal, so you don't need to go into great detail here. Your main purpose in writing the Synopsis is to grab the publisher's attention and hold it. Your mission is to sell him on the value and marketability of your book and the Synopsis is your second chance to do that. Your query letter was your first stab at this and it got you this far.

Jeff Herman, coauthor of *Write the Perfect Book Proposal* says that a Synopsis is your opportunity to have five minutes with a publisher. With that in mind, you know what you must do—write the most intriguing piece of work you've ever attempted.

Write your Synopsis in a style and tone similar to that of your proposed book. And be generous. Some authors feel they must hold back information. Some are afraid to reveal data and concepts for fear they will be stolen. Others feel it is good practice not to lay all of their cards on the table too soon.

Give facts and data where appropriate and where it will enhance your Synopsis. Provide examples and dialogue that you will use in the book, if you think it will give your project more clarity. I would encourage erring on the side of offering too much information as opposed to too little. Just watch that it is all important/pertinent information and not excessive drivel.

In fact, once you've written your Synopsis, tighten it up—get rid of excess words and phrases—just as you will your book once it is completed.

THE ONE SENTENCE CHALLENGE
I'd like to challenge you to come up with one sentence that describes your book. This will help you focus on your subject and it can become an excellent marketing tool.

Here's what I might say about my book, *Quest For Truth*. "It's the story of a non-believer's reluctant journey into the world of the supernatural through hypnosis, past-life regression and spiritual healing."

About my book, *Over 75 Good Ideas for Promoting Your Book*, I might describe it as: "A collection of low and no cost ideas for promoting your book."

For this book, *How to Write a Successful Book Proposal in 8 Days or Less,* I might say, "The ultimate pocket-sized book designed to teach hopeful authors how to write a successful book proposal." Or, "A definitive, no nonsense guide to writing a winning book proposal."

Try this with your book. It's not easy to envelope the entire scope of your book into one or even two sentences. But it is an excellent exercise. And if you can't do it, perhaps you need to reconsider the focus of your book.

A Synopsis is one to one and a half pages single-spaced. While it is recommended that the remainder of the book proposal be double-spaced, I don't always comply. It doesn't make sense to double-space the About the Author, for example, where you may include lists of credits and previously published books. The only parts of the book proposal that I always double-space are the Sample Chapters.

In the meantime, have you been researching appropriate publishers/ agents? Most of us begin with the most prestigious publishing houses. When that doesn't pan out, we start working down. Remember, that publishers such as Harper Collins, Scribner (Simon and Schuster), Ballantine (Random House), Bantam, Doubleday, etc. require that you have an agent before contacting them. If you are targeting a major publisher for your work, you might start seeking an appropriate agent.

Find agents listed in *Writer's Market, Literary Market Place* and online at www.aar-online.org.

A legitimate agent does not charge a reading fee. Agents make their money from the sale of your manuscript. However, they may charge small fees for copying.

GOOD NEWS ABOUT PUBLISHERS
There are hundreds of good publishers that prefer to deal directly with the author and who will provide you with the same exposure that any of the "big boys" will. And remember, even the largest publishers expect the author to help promote his/her book.

There are 300 publishers for biographies listed in *Writer's Market* and only a few of them are mega publishers. There are nearly 400 listings for books relating to history, about 100 publishers for creative nonfiction, 150 publishers of books on psychology, nearly 150 publishers for literary books, nearly 200 publishers of juvenile books, over 200 who publish how-tos and 300 publishers for scientific/technology books. In today's publishing climate, with so many new publishers cropping up, the opportunities seem boundless. In fact, according to Dan Poynter, self-publishing guru and keeper of industry statistics, there are somewhere around 80,000 publishers currently in America. Of course, this figure includes independent (self) publishers.

ASSIGNMENT
Start writing your Synopsis.
Write a one-sentence description of your book.

EXAMPLE OF A SUCCESSFUL SYNOPSIS

Youth Mentoring: Your Gift to the Next Generation
By Patricia Fry

(Note: The publisher changed the title to:
Youth Mentoring, Sharing Your Gifts With the Future)

The statement, "It takes a whole village to raise a child" was never more true than today. More children come from broken homes. They spend more time either in daycare or home alone while their parents work. Fewer children have the day-to-day support of extended family members. And neighborhoods lack the networking systems that once helped to keep our youngsters safe.

The book I propose will guide readers in becoming a positive influence by mentoring a child within their family or within their community. Through anecdotes, examples, success stories, tips, information and guidelines this book will teach and encourage men and women to take on the role of youth mentor to one child or several.

The Search Institute of Minneapolis has defined forty developmental assets that children need in order for them to flourish. These assets include family support, relationships with other adults, caring neighbors, positive school climate, the opportunity to give service to others, a sense of feeling safe, involvement in creative activities, a sense of purpose and a spiritual base. Studies show that the average youngster experiences only eighteen of the forty and as few as eight percent experience thirty-five to forty of these developmental assets.

We all know what happens when a child lacks the appropriate adult involvement, support and encouragement represented by these developmental assets. He does not thrive. He'll typically do poorly in school. He'll have behavior problems. He may show signs of depression. Children who fall into a pattern of drug abuse, promiscuity and violence, typically lack numbers of these developmental assets. Sadly, the fastest growing crime in America today is children killing children.

What does it take to reverse this horrifying trend? It can start with just one adult expressing an interest in just one youth. Yes, a solution for some young people is a mentor—a positive association with an adult other than his/her parents.

Even the most conscientious parents sometimes need help. Many of them are stressed to the max by the pressures of parenting and societal obligations. Add to that the need to earn a living and you have parents who are overwhelmed.

According to the Department of Labor, in 1995, nearly seventy percent of all mothers with children under the age of 18 worked. Over sixty-two percent of mothers with children under 6 work. America's young children are spending a lot of time in daycare. They're being raised by someone outside the family—learning the values of virtual strangers.

A recent study reveals that eighty-four percent of children by the age of 6 have spent time in some form of daycare. The same study declares that the more time kids spend in daycare, the more aggressive they become and the more behavior problems they have.

When these children reach the age of 8, 9 or 10, they become latchkey kids. Do you know how latchkey kids typically spend their afternoons? They are safely locked inside their homes watching TV or playing video games and eating junk food. The result is a decline in the overall fitness of our children and an increase in childhood obesity. According to a recent study, twenty-two percent of children between the ages of 12 and 17 are considered obese. What they're feeding their minds is another matter that obviously needs attention.

Those children who are allowed to roam the neighborhood after school without adult supervision are at risk of getting into trouble. The fact is that more vandalism, shoplifting, underage drinking, drug use and other crimes perpetuated by the younger set occur between 2 and 6 p.m. on school days.

The American family is in trouble. Fatherless boys are looking for fathers. Those who don't find a father figure in a relative, a teacher or a church leader, are at risk of joining gangs in search of one. Father-lack affects girls, too. Teen girls, feeling unloved and abandoned by their fathers, often become teen moms.

Our children's most valuable supportive links are no longer available to them. Gone is the American dream that includes the traditional two-parent family: one full-time parent and one breadwinner who also contributes strong physical and emotional support to the family. Many of our children have been emotionally and physically abandoned by career-driven, divorcing and drug/alcohol addicted parents.

Children don't feel nurtured by or safe in their neighborhoods, because most of their neighbors are strangers they see only in passing.

And we're even losing our sense of belonging through extended family support. Few kids can just hang out with grandpa after a tough day at school. Grandpa is likely either living in a retirement community miles away in a milder climate or pursuing his own personal adventure. Grandma isn't around to offer her grandchildren a safe haven, a fresh baked batch of cookies or her expertise in designing a Halloween costume. She's more apt to be running her own company or running a marathon.

The bottom line is that America's children are in crisis and we can help. This book is for those adults who are already mentoring a child either formally or informally and want more information, support and help in their endeavor. It's for the educator, religious leader and community leader who want to do more to help children and need additional guidance. It's for those who are ready to give something back to society and want to do it through our children. It will assist folks who already spend time with their grandchildren or kids in the neighborhood and who want additional inspiration and ideas for successful mentoring. And it's for those who, perhaps, see a problem developing with children in their community or neighborhood and they want to get involved but don't know how. This book is for every adult who cares about kids.

Book Proposal Class

3

THE SYNOPSIS, CONTINUED

We are still working on the Synopsis. Writing a Synopsis is not a walk in the park. But, the good news is that once you've completed it, you can go take that walk in the park. (Grin.) Actually, once you've completed your Synopsis, you will have material for your query letter and you have the preface or introduction for your book. You also have a clearer idea of your book focus. Is this becoming more apparent to you as you work on your Synopsis?

I created these notes based on the questions and material I received from my book proposal class students during week two.

1: Most authors find that organizing their book is one of the hardest parts of the whole writing process. Organization can also be a challenge in writing a synopsis. Make sure that you have organized your synopsis in the most logical manner.

2: Is your first sentence attention-grabbing? Imagine that you are a very busy publisher and you're seeing the Synopsis for the first time. What is your first impression? Are you intrigued? Are you interested enough to keep reading?

3: Keep it simple. Avoid long, cumbersome sentences like the plague. This is no time to get fancy or to flaunt your mastery of the English language. In order to dazzle a publisher, he first must understand

22

what you're saying. Write as if you're explaining this to someone from outer space.

4: Use active rather than passive sentences. Example:
Passive: The game was won by the Bluebirds.
Active: The Bluebirds won the game.

Passive: A decision to adjourn was made by the president.
Active: The president adjourned the meeting.

5: Write a one-sentence description of your book. This will help you to find your focus for the Synopsis.

6: For those of you who have a story to tell, don't try to tell the whole story in the Synopsis. Just outline the basic storyline, include something about the prominent players in the story and add an example or two from the story.

7: For those of you with nonfiction books, include statistics in your Synopsis and introduce the experts you'll be quoting.

8: Don't try to hide things from the publisher. While I urge you to give brief and succinct descriptions, avoid playing peek-a-boo games. Don't keep the publisher in suspense. Be straightforward.

9: Where you have several points to make, consider using bullets. For example: "In my book, *Doggie Dress-Up*, I will cover the following:
- Who, in general, dress their dogs?
- Why do people dress their dogs?
- Which celebrities parade dogs wearing clothes?
- What dog types are most often subjected to the practice of dressing up?
- What is the most popular doggie dress-up style?
- What are some of the most outlandish outfits worn by dogs?
- Where can one find doggie outfits?"

10: Make a strong statement at the end of your Synopsis indicating your assuredness that the publisher will consider publishing your manuscript. For example:

Instead of, "I hope you find this manuscript suitable for publication." Or "I would love it if you decide to publish this." Or "Thank you for your time." Say, "This book will be a valuable asset to the dog owner who is on the fence about investing in a wardrobe for his dog." Or "I envision this book being warmly received by children and parents everywhere."

In other words, put positive thoughts in the publisher's head.

ASSIGNMENT:
Continue fine-tuning your Synopsis

Book Proposal Class

4

YOUR MARKETING STRATEGIES

In these competitive times, the promotions portion of one's book proposal is among the most important aspects. A publisher wants to know that you have a grasp on your target audience and that you understand how to reach them. He also needs your assurance that you will help promote the book.

LOCATING YOUR TARGET AUDIENCE
Who is your target audience? Who are the primary readers for your book? What segment of the population did you have in mind when you conceived the idea for this book? Who did you want to help, educate, inform or entertain? And PLEASE do not say, "Everyone." Say this to a publisher and you will definitely receive a rejection letter. There is no such thing as a one-size-fits-all book. Even the world's best-selling book, the Bible, isn't embraced by all of humanity. Tell a publisher that your audience is everyone and you've just blown your professional cover.

Now get real. Who is your target audience? Let's use our *Doggie Dress Up* book as an example. Who would buy this book? Most likely, they are people who currently dress their dogs, people who sell canine clothing and people who would like to dress up their dogs, right? Throw in a few dog owners who are curious about such things and add them all up. There's your potential target audience.

25

For a book on writing and publishing you could state the following statistic, "Nearly eighty-one percent of the population believe they have a book in them and there are around six million manuscripts circulating through publishing companies in any given year." This certainly indicates a large enough audience to support a book on authorship.

For my youth mentoring book, I might remind the publisher that there are twenty-three million children who go to bed each night without a father in the home and that many of those children could use a mentor.

I might state that there are over two million mentors currently working with children and that those mentors could use a book that offers tips and activities for mentors. There are another fifteen million children who say that they would like to have a mentor. This establishes a need for a book that will encourage mentoring and, in fact, shows men and women who want to help, how to participate.

Last year at a book festival, an author came to me asking for help promoting his book. It was a scientific view designed to disprove the concept of God. Putting my prejudices aside, I asked the author, "Who is your target audience?" He quickly responded, "Everyone." I said, "Everyone will want to read this book?" And he said, "Everyone should read this book."

I urged him to think again about who would *want* to read this book and where the author might find them. I suggested that people with the same view as his would be most likely to purchase this book. He agreed. I said, "Then, you will find readers for your book at the same places you frequent—the same Web sites, the same meetings and the same social circles. These people read the sort of magazines you read and subscribe to the same newsletters. That's where you'll find your audience."

Of course, he dreamed of bookstore managers eagerly scooping up his book by the box load and stocking them front and center where every curiosity seeker would find them. And this is simply not going to happen unless the book is published by a mega, large or medium publisher. Bookstores generally won't stock self-published or POD published books. I've even known of traditional royalty publishers who couldn't get their books into bookstores.

Determine your target audience before you ever begin to write your book. Like I said earlier, the process of developing a Book Proposal might cause you to change your focus and one reason to shift gears is to attract a larger audience.

For example, a book designed to teach summer gardening techniques in Northern California would draw a larger audience if it were expanded to cover all of the seasons in the entire northwest. A book teaching senior citizens to fly would have a wider appeal if it included beginning pilots of all ages and a section on how to purchase your first plane.

YOUR PROMOTIONAL PLAN

What can you offer the publisher in the way of your expertise toward promoting this book? What are some of your ideas? Where do you see it being sold? How can you participate in going after sales?

I interview publishers regularly for the *SPAWN Market Update* posted monthly at the SPAWN Web site member area. (That's Small Publishers, Artists and Writers Network— spawn.org.) When I ask these publishers what sort of authors they most like working with, they almost always mention those with time, energy, ideas, the ability and the WILLINGNESS to promote their own books.

THE BOOKSTORE

Most authors expect to see their book sold through bookstores. Unfortunately, only a fraction of the books published each year ever land on bookstore shelves. A well-known publisher with a good track record can usually get your book into bookstores. Even you can persuade bookstore managers to carry your book if you can initiate enough sales to make it worth their while. Get a gig on Oprah or Montel, for example. Arrange for widespread newspaper publicity.

When customers come in by the droves and start requesting your book, bookstore owners will carry it.

But are you sure that bookstores are the best outlet for your books? Just look at the competition. Even someone walking into a bookstore expressly to purchase your book (which, if it's listed in *Books In Print* can be ordered), is easily swayed to purchase one that's in stock.

Most book promotion experts and successful book promotion professionals agree that specialty stores are more lucrative outlets for many books than traditional bookstores. So, in your proposal, you might list some of the types of stores that could be a match for your particular book—an automotive shop for a book on vintage cars, for example; hospital gift shops, baby stores and maternity shops for a parenting book and pet shops, feed stores and veterinarian offices for a book on animal behavior or pet-related poems.

EXAMPLES FROM MY BOOK PROPOSAL
Here are some of the promotional ideas I offered the publisher in my book proposal for *Youth Mentoring, Sharing Your Gifts With the Future* (Liguori Publications, 2004). I said that I would be available to promote it through book signings and speaking engagements to civic organizations, youth foundations, clergy, educator's groups and so forth. I said that I would send press releases and offer follow up to the seventy-five or so organizations and agencies I included in my resource list. I said that I would do radio and TV spots as well as write articles for magazines. I listed some of the magazines that might publish an article on this topic and their circulation (information available in *Writer's Market*). I promised to promote the book on my Web site. I also said that I would solicit book reviews in appropriate magazines, newsletters and Web sites related to youth-oriented clubs and organizations. I told them that I envisioned this book being sold through traditional and religious bookstores and gift shops as well as catalogs for educators, religious leaders and family counselors.

As a measure of proof, I shared with the publisher some of my credentials and experiences related to public speaking, book tours, media interviews and so forth. It's important that the publisher have something to hang his hat on—that he is fairly well convinced that you are not just blowing in the wind.

WHAT EXPERTISE CAN YOU OFFER?

Perhaps you're willing to give seminars on the topic of your book. If so, state this in your book proposal. Would articles in key publications be a good way to sell this book? Are you willing to solicit assignments and write those articles? Be sure to tell this to the publisher.

What are your strengths—public speaking, being organized enough to send out press releases regularly, planning and running seminars? Talk about your background and expertise. I've been involved with Toastmasters for a number of years and frequently do public speaking. I typically include this in the promotion section of my book proposals. I also mention my affiliations that might help in the promotion of my book—magazines that I write for regularly, organizations that I belong to, etc.

YOUR BOOK AS A PREMIUM ITEM

Perhaps your book would make a good premium item. Suggest this to the publisher. Companies often purchase large numbers of books to give away to customers. For example, a historical novel might be of interest to a bank or other large business in the area where the story takes place. A local history book might appeal to the school district, historical society, museum and libraries in this place. They might offer to purchase your book at a discount as a fund raiser.

A scientific book could be a premium item, too—for businesses related to the topic, perhaps. And this book could be marketed through museum gift shops, appropriate scientific organizations and Web sites, schools as well as children's bookstores.

A book related to art and to children might be a good premium item for banks, law firms, large companies that manufacture art supplies and so forth. This book could also be sold through children's bookstores, art supply stores, gift shops and catalogs of books for educators, artists, psychologists.

YOUR MAILING LIST
Create a mailing list. Start now adding to your mailing list. Add family, friends, acquaintances, your kids' teachers, your dry cleaner, coworkers, fellow volunteers, people you know from the gym, former classmates. You get the idea. Collect business cards and brochures, especially from folks with whom you've discussed your book and who seem even remotely interested. When your book comes out, send each of them an announcement and an order form and/or an invitation to a book signing.

Make time to go through your local telephone directory and online directories for other communities. Highlight organizations and companies that might be interested in your book. For my youth mentoring book, I contacted family counselors, schools, mentoring organizations, civic organizations and youth organizations.

PLAN A SUCCESSFUL BOOK SIGNING
Most new authors see dollar signs and prominence when they envision their first book signing. In reality, most book signings generate little acknowledgement and few sales. You have the power to change this reality by planning ahead.

The typical author signing results in anywhere from 0 to 8 book sales. One of my clients was the guest author at a very small, local bookstore recently and he sold over fifty copies of his $24.95 true crime book. How? He arranged to be interviewed in two local newspapers so that the articles appeared during the week of the event. He sent custom-made postcard invitations to his entire mailing list. He made sure that there were posters noting his signing displayed prominently in the store. He told everyone he talked to about the event. And he gave the bookstore manager flyers to be included with each purchase during the weeks prior to the signing.

Perhaps you are beginning to see the importance of establishing and maintaining a complete and up-to-date mailing list.

BOOKSIGNING TIPS FOR AUTHORS
This article first appeared on the SPAWN Web site.
Once you're over the thrill of holding your latest published book in your hands, it's time to get down to the business of selling it. And a favorite promotional activity for most authors is the book signing.

Contrary to popular belief, people don't typically swarm authors at these events and purchase hundreds or thousands of copies of their books. An unknown author might sell just a handful of books if she's lucky. But, her success rate increases with her efforts. Here are a few dos and don'ts that will help make your next book signing more successful.

1: Don't wait for an invitation. Take the initiative and approach the managers of businesses related to your book topic and local bookstores. Offer to give a presentation or to sign books for their customers.

If the subject of your book lends itself to demonstrations, plan one for this event. Debbie Puente is the author of *Elegantly Easy Crème Brulee and Other Custard Desserts*. People attending her book signings are frequently treated to a demonstration and a sample. Teddy Colbert, author of *The Living Wreath*, often shares her expertise in making succulent wreaths, when she signs her book at nurseries and garden shops.

I sell more books at signings where I give presentations. I like to introduce myself and my book, give a brief overview and then I generally answer audience questions.

Eighteen days before the event:

2: Send Press Releases with a photograph of yourself or your book cover to all newspapers within a forty-mile radius. Relate the particulars of the planned event, write about your book and include your bio. Give your phone number. An editor may want to contact you for more information.

3: Make calls and send postcards and emails to friends, acquaintances, business associates and club affiliates inviting them to your signing. Post flyers on bulletin boards where you work and in public places. Have notices placed in appropriate company and club newsletters and bulletins.

Ten days in advance of the event:

4: Find out if the store plans to design posters and flyers to advertise your signing. If not, do this yourself and deliver them to the store a week in advance of the event. Ask the manager to include a flyer with each purchase during the week prior to your event.

5: Offer to design a store display of your books.

One week in advance of the event:

6: Know ahead of time what to expect: Will you have a microphone? Podium? Table at which to sit for signing? Or will you have to arrange for these things yourself?

7: Make sure the store has enough books in stock.

The day of the event.

8: Dress to stand out in a crowd, but not so dramatically as to distract from your presentation.

9: Be prompt. Arriving a little early won't hurt and it will give you time to settle in.

10: Bring handouts—a relating article or a sample chapter, for example. When I'm signing my book, *Quest For Truth,* I hand out my article on Meditation Walking. When the event features *The Mainland Luau*, I give away a recipe.

11: Reach out to people, don't wait for them to come to you. Hand copies of your book to folks in the audience or who visit your signing table. If you're sitting all alone, walk around the store and strike up a conversation with customers. Hand a copy of your book to them. Someone is more apt to purchase something they've held in their hands.

12: Keep track of the number of books you autograph in case there is a discrepancy.

After the event:

13: Send a note of thanks to the store manager and staff.

14: Attend other signings and note what works and what doesn't.

15: Arrange more book signings, presentations and demonstrations at bookstores and/or specialty stores. Consider a combined signing with other authors. This should be someone whose book compliments your own, but doesn't compete with it. A book of animal-related poems and a novel about a dog might entice the same buyers. You could promote your book on writing thank you notes along with one featuring how to make paper products. Another compatible combination might be a book on marketing web site businesses and one featuring how to gear up for a job in technology.

16: Realize that signings and presentations will rarely exceed your expectations and hardly ever meet your highest goals. But *anytime* you are given the opportunity for this sort of free publicity, you are making headway in your promotional effort.

> Always think *exposure* instead of sales, and you'll never be disappointed.

DEVELOP A PROJECT TO PROMOTE YOUR BOOK
Create a project to promote your book. This would definitely impress the publisher. I know a man who wrote a novel featuring the life and times of a homeless couple. He could start a service or charity for homeless people in his area to help promote his book. How does that work? When you are doing good work, this is newsworthy. When

you get press, always mention your book. I'm in California and I once read an article in a local newspaper about a young girl who serves homemade sandwiches to the homeless in a park somewhere in the Midwest every Sunday after church. If she had a book to promote, it would have been mentioned in this article.

For a book related to the arts, form an arts organization, run a contest for young artists or design a series of classes for artists.

Produce a newsletter. If you establish a newsletter related to the theme of your book, this will please a publisher. Remember, though, people are turned off by blatant advertisements. You must strive to offer genuine information and resources for readers. Promoting your book is secondary. Your expertise and generosity will sell books.

PROVE YOURSELF

I've worked with hopeful authors who list some pretty ambitious promotional projects in their book proposals. One of them planned a fifty-city tour to promote his book. I asked him where his tour would take him and what he would do once he got there. He hadn't thought that far ahead. And that's too bad, because a publisher wants specifics, not empty promises. He wants to know where you plan to tour, what sort of arrangements you've made, what you've done to attract a good crowd, who you're contacts are and when you'll be starting your book tour.

This client might say in his book proposal, for example, "I'm planning a tour of fifty cities in the northeast during the fall of 2007. I lived in that area most of my life and have connections in several school districts and library systems there. I was on the school board in Bar Harbor, Maine for three years and I have worked in libraries in three eastern states."

One woman wrote in her book proposal that she would do workshops to promote her book. I asked if she had any previous experience presenting workshops or speaking in public. She said, "No, but it can't be that hard." Well, that's not the point. A publisher is more impressed with a track record than smoke dreams. What he wants to hear is, "I've been presenting workshops and speaking at conferences related to the subject of my proposed book for the last ten years." I would also recommend that this author mention a few of her more successful presentations—the venue and the number of people in attendance.

I often suggest to people that they promote their book before it's a book and there are a number of ways to do this:

PROMOTE YOUR BOOK BEFORE IT'S A BOOK

If you are self-publishing your book, make sure that it has what it needs to be sold through retail outlets—an ISBN (International Standard Book Number), bar code, cataloguing material used by libraries, a listing in *Books in Print* and appropriate binding. (Some bookstores and libraries won't accept a saddle-stitched book or one that's spiral bound.)

Build marketing potential into your book. When I wrote the Ojai Valley history, I interviewed dozens of people and mentioned all of them in the book. Practically everyone likes to see his name in print and will most likely buy one or more copies of the book.

Here are some ideas for involving people in your book. Ask experts in the field of your subject to write testimonials for the back cover. Quote experts in the text. Mention agencies and organizations in your resource list. Each of these people is a potential customer. And, perhaps some of the organizations listed in the book will use it to promote their own causes.

For example, let's say you're writing a novel that includes a character with diabetes or a book on healthcare that features a section on diabetes. The American Diabetes Association might be interested in helping you promote the book through their organization.

Whether your book is of a scientific nature, will appeal to artists, is important to psychologists or significant to history buffs, you can build promotional opportunities into your book. All you have to do is include pertinent resources, quote experts in the field and/or request that high profile people write testimonials for your back cover.

To get expert participation, simply identify your experts and contact them in a professional, business-like manner. Be sensitive to their busy schedules. Be prepared with your questions or request when you make contact. If you want a testimonial, ask the individual for permission to send the entire manuscript for them to review or, perhaps, he/she will require just your synopsis, your book proposal or the chapter related to his or her expertise. If you want to quote someone, call and ask for a telephone or face-to-face interview at their convenience. But have your questions prepared before you make that call in case they are willing to respond at that moment. Or you could make arrangements to do an email interview. You might be surprised at how willing most experts and high profile people are to work with an author who is professional, business-like and sensitive to issues of time. Just make everything as easy and convenient for them as you can.

END NOTES
Your promotion section should fit on one page because you're going to condense each of your promotional ideas. There is no law against going over one page if you can come up with enough promotional ideas and really concrete examples. You want to appear organized and clear as to your promotional path. Listing possible ideas helter skelter will probably lose the publisher's interest. He/she will be more impressed by solid ideas, the specific action you plan to take and proof of your expertise and/or ability to carry them out.

ASSIGNMENT:
Write your promotions page.
- Try to include statistics that show the need for this book.
- State who your audience is.
- Suggest where this book might logically be sold.
- Outline what you are willing to do in order to promote this book.

> Read my book, *Over 75 Good Ideas for Promoting Your Book* to get some ideas for marketing your book. It's available at matilijapress.com for $6.50. In this book, I offer over seventy-five low and no cost ways to promote your book along with anecdotes and resources.

Never be so naïve as to believe that your book will sell itself. This is only true if your name is Bill Clinton or JK Rowling—however, you see these high profile authors on the promotions trail, too. You and your publisher will have to earn each and every sale you make. As Dan Poynter (the self-publishing guru) said in his testimonial on the back cover of my book, *Over 75 Good Ideas for Promoting Your Book,* "Writing the book is the tip of the iceberg; promoting it is the larger part under the water. And whether you sell out to a publisher or publish yourself, the author must do the promotion. Fortunately, you are not alone. This book is a goldmine of promotion ideas, encouragement and leads." Dan Poynter, *The Self-Publishing Manual.*

SAMPLE PROMOTIONS SECTION
This is from the successful book proposal for my book, *The Right Way to Write, Publish and Sell Your Book.*

Marketing Strategies
I am already in promotion mode when it comes to my writing/publishing-related books. I will continue on the course I have set which includes, promoting this book through the SPAWN Web site and newsletter and in my numerous email communications with SPAWN members and visitors to the site. I will announce the book in various writing-related newsletters and Web sites such as *Absolute Write, Writing-World, Writer's Weekly, NAWW newsletter, Writing for Dollars, Spannet, Writer's Connection, Working Writer Newsletter, Writer's Review* and others. I'll promote the book in my tagline accompanying articles published in *Writer's Digest Magazine, Freelance Writer's Report, Writer's Journal, Canadian Author* and so forth.

I write the monthly SPAWN Market Update and also use this publication as a means to promote my writing/publishing-related books.

To discover the magnitude of promo I've done for my other writing books, do a Google search. Even doing a refined search—using quotation marks around *Successful Writer's Handbook*—you'll receive 1,400 hits, 289 for *Over 75 Good Ideas for Promoting Your Book* and over 210,000 when typing in my name.

I will arrange for book reviews on writing-related sites as well as in magazines and newsletters. I've had approximately 100 reviews for my writing books in recent years.

I also promote my writing books through speaking engagements. In February of 2004, I spoke at the Much Ado About Books event in Jacksonville, FL and at the National Association of Women Writers conference in TX. I spoke at the Central Coast Book Festival in San Luis Obispo, CA in September and the Meet Me in St. Louis Book Festival in MO in October.

I was invited to speak at the Toastmasters International convention last year in Reno, however, I had to cancel due to a broken foot. I also canceled an invitation to speak in NY for the Society for Professional Journalists because of the injury. I'm on their agenda for 2006. This year, I'm doing workshops in St. Louis, MO, Los Angeles, CA and Simi Valley, CA.

I have applied for speaking opportunities in 2006 at book festivals and writers' conferences in Las Vegas, Phoenix, Flagstaff, Illinois, Wisconsin, Virginia, Florida, San Diego and Los Angeles.

Through SPAWN, we frequently purchase booths at book festivals where I typically sell numbers of my writing/publishing-related books. We generally secure booths at the Santa Barbara Book Festival, Los Angeles Times Festival of Books, Austin (TX) Book Festival, Meet Me In St. Louis Festival of Books and the Central Coast Book Festival. We had three booths at the gigantic Los Angeles Times Book Festival this year.

I have a Web site through which I promote my books. www.matilijapress.com. I am also available for any tours or speaking engagements that you might arrange.

Book Proposal Class

5

MARKET ANALYSIS COMPETITIVE WORKS

Today, I want you to prepare a Market Analysis or Comparison of Competitive Works.

The purpose of this part of the book proposal is to demonstrate to the publisher that your book is needed. You must show him that your book will fill a void or that there is a market for a book of this type.

It used to be that publishers knew what books were out there and what was needed. A publisher who didn't, would do the research to determine whether there was a need for another book on gardening or Yoga or baseball card collecting. Now the publisher relies on you, the author, to do that research. The publisher wants your feedback about the current market as it relates to your book subject. Is there room for another book like yours or is the market saturated? What makes your book different than the books already available on this topic? It is up to you to find out and to share this information with the publisher.

Sometimes during this research, an author will decide to shift gears— to change the focus or the scope of his/her book.

Let's say that you're writing a book on how to groom a dog. While researching competitive works, you might find scads of books about dog grooming in general, but few to help groomers with specific types of dogs. Based on this information, you might decide to write, instead, a book on how to groom the silky, yorky and other small, long-hair terriers. Or you may choose to produce a book featuring a collection of humorous stories from dog groomers.

Start your search by looking for books on the subject of your book. Search Amazon.com and your local mega-bookstore. Do a Google search to locate obscure books that are out there but not sold in the usual channels. Read those books that sound most similar to your own. At least read the description of these books and look at the table of contents. Discover the scope and focus of these books and determine how yours differs.

The publisher wants to know what makes your book different—special. What specific value or benefit does your book offer the reader? Why will a consumer purchase your book instead of the others? It is necessary that you are absolutely clear as to why your book is different and why it should be published. And it is up to you to convince the publisher.

It's considered unprofessional and naïve to tell a publisher that there is nothing out there like your book. If that's so (and it's highly unlikely) maybe there's a reason why no one has written a book on this subject. Ideally, you want to write a book on a popular or current topic but with a different twist. Dieting, for example, is a hot topic. I happen to know that there were 426 new diet books published in 2004. But a publisher will be interested in your book on dieting only if you offer a fresh focus. *Have Sex and Lose Weight,* for example. Or *The Primary Color Diet* (lose weight eating only foods in the primary colors).

Sometimes, however, you really can't find other books like the one you are pitching. No one else has ever written a book on cow pies and other fuel for campfires. You truly cannot locate another book of bubblegum recipes. No one else is likely to write a book featuring your life story as a short-order cook. And you probably won't find a publisher for these books, either. If you really want to produce an obscure book like these, self-publishing is probably the way to go. But be realistic. Print only the small number that you might give away to immediate family and sell to a few eccentrics at eBay.

Here's what I wrote in my Market Analysis for my youth mentoring book.

SAMPLE MARKET ANALYSIS
This is from my successful book proposal for *Youth Mentoring, Sharing your Gifts With the Future.*

My research failed to reveal any books like the one I propose. Most books on mentoring today reflect adult-to-adult mentoring in the business world. Some of those listed below have more religious leanings than is probably comfortable among mainstream readers. While I plan to embrace a spiritual perspective in my book, it will not be overly religious in tone.

Through research, I found books written for people who want to help highly troubled teens. My book is designed to encourage and assist adults in mentoring kids **before** their life spirals out of control.

I also located books for organizations and individuals who want to establish a mentor program for youths. While I will touch on what it takes to start a program and I will include an extensive Resource List, the focus of my book is different. My book is designed to entice, encourage and guide readers who want to work formally or informally as a mentor for a child or children within their family, neighborhood or community.

Competitive Works
Intensive Caring: Practical Ways to Mentor Youth by William Hendricks (Group Publishing, 1998). This book has heavy religious overtones and would not be appropriate for the average reader who is looking for a more mainstream method of reaching a child.

Mentoring: Confidence in Finding a Mentor and Becoming One by Bobb Biehl (Broadman and Holman Publishers, 1997). This book features lifetime mentoring relationships. Biehl comes from a highly Christian perspective which may discourage some people from participating.

Big Questions, Worthy Dreams: Mentoring Young Adults in Their Search for Meaning, Purpose and Faith by Sharon Daloz Parks (Jossey-Bass, 2000).

This book features mentoring ideas for the young adult rather than the teen and mainly in the area of spirituality.

Mentoring and the Rites of Passage for Youth by Ralph Steele (Ralvon, 1998). This is a guide to parents, mentors and organizations who wish to start a mentor program.

Mentoring for Resiliency: Setting up Programs to Move Youth from Stressed to Success by Nan Henderson (2000). This book relies on the expertise of several contributing authors and focuses on information about mentoring and various programs. This is not a how-to.

At Risk: Bringing Hope to Hurting Teens by Scott Larsen (Group Publishing, 1999). This book is for those who are interested in working with intensely troubled kids.

> Choose books published within the last five years or so—the more recent, the better. However, if the books that relate are all older than that, by all means, use them as examples.

ASSIGNMENT

Today, I want you to begin your search for works similar to yours and provide an explanation for the publisher as to what makes your book needed and/or different.

Be genuine in choosing books to use in your comparative study. You might point out a book that is similar to yours and that is highly popular. If you can find out how many copies they've sold of this book, all the better. This will demonstrate a need for books of this type.

In the case of a biography, you can mention books written about this person and explain why yours is different. If these books are popular, mention that. If other books on this individual sold millions of copies, why wouldn't yours? You can also bring into play biographies on other people to use as a comparison—especially if these books are popular.

Where it is a totally new concept and there are truly very few books out there like it, as in a book related to an obscure scientific concept, state this and then find a book on another scientific topic that is similar to yours and that is selling well. You can tell the publisher that your book will be along those lines.

I would suggest comparing anywhere from four to half dozen competitive works.

Book Proposal Class

6

ABOUT THE AUTHOR

Another important part of the book proposal is the About the Author. The publisher wants to know who you are, what sort of writing experience you have and what qualifies you to write this book.

Fill half page to one and a half pages with your qualifications. What sort of writing have you done in the past? Have you had anything published? List your writing credits and experience. If you've had a lot of writing experience, mention those most similar to the project you're pitching. If you are a new writer, don't belabor your lack of experience. Share the fact that you are the newsletter editor for your church, mention the article you had published in a national gardening magazine and let your superb writing and organizational skills shine throughout your magnificent book proposal.

Share your qualifications to write this particular book. Is this your field of expertise? Perhaps you don't consider yourself an expert on the topic, but it is something you've been interested in for years. Play up your research skills and any involvement you've had within the realm of your subject. Maybe your book is about how to attract hummingbirds to a backyard garden. You may not be an ornithologist, a wild bird specialist, a breeder or even a bird park curator. However, you might have conducted a lifelong personal study of hummingbirds and have experimented for years to discover the plants and feeders that best support these tiny birds. Mention this. You could also mention that you have a library full of books on hummingbirds that would rival any ornithologist's collection. Include the fact that you have consulted hummingbird experts Lanny Chambers and Sheri Williamson for your book. And, if you are a member of a hummingbird migration checkpoint club in your state, say so.

Illustrate your ability to follow-through with major projects. When necessary and appropriate, I enclose letters of recommendation from former clients who hired me to do large, complicated projects for them. In order to convince a publisher of your abilities, you might say, "My sense of stick-to-itiveness and follow-through are evident in the success of the county-wide Environmental Days event I organized with a volunteer staff of thirty last fall. Commendation from the governor enclosed." Or "I'm executive director of BAM, a state-wide businesswoman's organization." Or "I head up a local volunteer literacy program for prisoners."

If you have other books in the works, mention them. Publishers want to know that if this book sells well, you can provide him with others. Remember, he is in this business to make money. This is his primary motivation. What information and materials can you provide him to convince him that your book is a sound investment?

Here's how I might start my About the Author: "I've been writing for publication for thirty-one years having contributed hundreds of articles to about 190 different magazines. (I will then list some of the magazines that relate to the topic of my book proposal.) I am also the author of twenty-two books including (and I will list those most relevant to the subject I am now pitching)."

I would then provide evidence of my expertise. If I was pitching my mentoring book, I would mention that I have been a formal mentor through the Ojai Valley Youth Foundation for three years and have been involved in neighborhood mentoring with some at-risk children over the past several years. I might list my experiences as a volunteer leader of a children's writing group and talk about my Write For Life program which I take into local schools. I would also say that I have

45

written several articles on mentoring and I would list the titles and magazines.

In my book proposal for a writing-related book, I would include my affiliation with SPAWN (Small Publishers, Artists and Writers Network), talk about the fact that I've taught seminars and online courses on various writing/publishing subjects (where, for whom, when), that I recently developed and taught a publishing course to 12 homeschoolers and so forth. I would also mention the other writing-related books I have to my credit and those that I plan to complete and produce at a later date.

ASSIGNMENT
Write your About the Author page. While it seems as though this would be the easiest part of the Book Proposal after the title page, writing the About the Author is often a real struggle for authors. I remember having the same struggle when I was starting out in this profession over thirty years ago. I recall agonizing over even a thirty or 100-word bio. While I don't want you to fabricate or even exaggerate too much, I suggest, again, that you focus on the publisher. What will/won't get his attention or impress him? Remember what I told you above—the publisher wants to know what qualifies you to write this book—what is your expertise in this subject? Can you write this book? How can you prove to the publisher that you have the skill and sense of follow-through to actually complete the project?

EXAMPLE OF ABOUT THE AUTHOR
From *The Right Way to Write, Publish and Sell Your Book*

I've been writing for publication for over thirty years, having contributed hundreds of articles to about 190 different magazines. My articles have appeared in *Writer's Digest, Authorship, Writer's Journal, Freelance Writer's Report, Canadian Author, The World and I, Entrepreneur Magazine, Pages, Cat Fancy, Los Angeles Times, Kiwanis Magazine, Your Health, The Artist's Magazine* and many other magazines. My writing/publishing-related articles, to date, number around 200.

I'm the author of twenty-two books. (See list of published books and works in progress next page.)

I helped to organize the nine-year-old networking organization, SPAWN (Small Publishers, Artists and Writers Network). I'm currently the president.

I work with clients on their writing projects. I've done editing for clients, ghostwriting, book proposal-writing, promotion consultations and I've helped clients find publishers for their projects. One client just landed a contract with Houghton Mifflin.

I teach online classes for Writing-World and on my own. I taught a book proposal class last year. This year I'm also teaching article-writing and self-publishing courses. My seminar topics include Book Promotion 101, How to write articles for magazines, self-publishing topics. (See list of conferences in Marketing Section.) I also work with young writers. Earlier this year, I led a group of twelve homeschoolers in an 8-week course that resulted in a 136-page published book of their works which the students also designed.

I write the monthly *SPAWN Market Update* for the SPAWN Web site. Through this eight to fourteen-page newsletter, I report on industry news. In order to stay current, I must be constantly in research mode—aware of trends and events. I also interview publishers and agents. I've completed fifty-one editions of the *Market Update*.

While I have written on a number of topics over the years, there is nothing that I know better or love more than the subject of writing and publishing. It's obvious that I'm the right person to write this book. Not only does it include material that I know, but I have numerous contacts with other experts and the ability, contacts and energy to promote this book through a number of channels.

Book Titles:

Hints For the Backyard Rider – A.S. Barnes, 1978 (out of print)
The Ojai Valley: An Illustrated History (a 360-page comprehensive local history) – Matilija Press, 1983; 2nd printing (revised) 1999.

Nordhoff Cemetery: Book One, Matilija Press, 1992

A Thread to Hold, The Story of Ojai Valley School (a 325-page comprehensive history of a local, world-known, 80-year-old private school) – Fithian Press, 1996

The Mainland Luau: How to Capture the flavor of Hawaii in Your Own Backyard – Matilija Press, 1996; 2nd printing, 1997 (3rd printing by Island Heritage)

Entertaining Hawaiian Style — Island Heritage Publishing, 1999

Quest For Truth, A Journey of the Soul – Matilija Press, 1996

Creative Grandparenting Across the Miles, Ideas for Sharing Love, Faith and Family Traditions – Liguori Publications, 1997.

A Writer's Guide to Magazine Articles for Book Promotion and Profit – Matilija Press, 2000.

Over 75 Good Ideas for Promoting Your Book –Matilija Press, 2000

Write On! Journal-keeping for Teens — Liguori Publications, July, 2001.

The Successful Writer's Handbook – Matilija Press 2002. An ebook featuring Fry's best writing-related articles.

Nordhoff Cemetery: Book Two, Matilija Press, 2003

The Successful Writer's Handbook – Matilija Press, 2003. Revised book published in print.

Young Writer's Handbook – Matilija Press, 2003

Youth Mentoring, Sharing Your Gifts With the Future (Liguori Publications, 2004)

6 private and corporate generated publications

Note: Matilija Press is the author's publishing company.

Books in the Works:

Fatherhood and Fathering: The Ultimate Guide For Today's Dad. This book is complete.

The Grandparent's Survival Guide. A book for the millennium grandparent.

Hope For Parents and Teens: Stop Bickering and Start Understanding: A unique book of hope for both parents and teens— parents read it from the front to the middle and the teen turns it over and reads it from the back to the middle.

The Inner Vacation: How to Go Away and Return Really Refreshed and Recharged. Alone But Not Lonely: Keys to Healthy, Happy, Solitary Living.
Shift Your Life to the Next Level Through Your Own Creativity. A guide to living in the now.
Write From the Heart: Journal to Find Your True Path
7 Stages of Writing, From Infatuation to your Final Chapter

Book Proposal Class

7

CHAPTER OUTLINE

You've written a synopsis or an overview of your book, created a promotional plan, prepared a market analysis of your book and worked on your About the Author. Now it is time to show the potential publisher that you actually have a book by writing a Chapter Outline. This is your moment of truth. If you cannot list at least five or six stand-alone chapters and describe them, you probably don't have a book, at all.

The Chapter Outline will help the publisher understand the flow of your proposed book. He/she will learn whether your attempt at organizing the book makes logical sense and whether your book has substance and relevance.

There are probably numerous ways to break your book idea down into chapters. Here's how I do it for my nonfiction books. I go over the material I've collected for the book—the interviews, data, statistics, my notes and other research. I separate this material into topics and subtopics. I create a file folder for each topic and/or subtopic. These eventually become my chapters.

In the case of my little seventy-page book on long-distance grandparenting, I created ten chapters divided in this way—how to communicate with grandkids by telephone, creative correspondence, fun with electronic communication, great gifts for long-distance grandkids, when you visit the grandchildren, when the grandchildren visit you, traveling with grandkids, meaningful family traditions, how to be a good role model even at a distance and I conclude with a chapter on the grandparent-parent connection and how important a positive one is to the children.

When I was organizing the chapters for this book, I changed my mind several times. I must have moved information and data from folder to folder a dozen times before settling on a logical chapter flow.

How do you know when you are not on the right track? When one file folder (representing a chapter) is overflowing and others have just a wisp of paper inside. This is an indication that maybe your chapters are not well balanced.

For the grandparenting book, I originally planned a chapter on communicating with your grandchildren. It soon became apparent, however, that there was enough material in this file folder to create three chapters (telephone communication, communicating by mail and communicating electronically). I originally had a chapter planned featuring holiday traditions. I came to realize, however, that there are many kinds of family traditions and I broadened the scope of that concept creating a chapter comprising meaningful family traditions and how to maintain them even at a distance.

It took me five years to research for and write *The Ojai Valley: An Illustrated History*. Now that was a bear of a project to organize. I wasn't sure whether to present the material chronologically, by subject (farming in the valley, early churches, etc) or by featuring the pioneers who shaped the valley. I ended up doing all three. I probably spent a good few weeks just organizing the twenty-one chapters over the subsequent 358 pages. And even after I started writing the book, I was still making chapter changes.

How did I use all three methods? I start the book with the geology of the valley, work through each historical event as they occurred while stopping to introduce various pioneers and their contributions along the way. I have a separate section where I focus on the history of the various communities within this valley. I feel that the organization in this book is appropriate and I've never had anyone offer anything but praise for this work in its twenty-one year existence.

While you're working on your chapter outline, don't be surprised if your book project begins to change right before your eyes. That is why you are preparing a book proposal—in order to work out any bugs before presenting your wonderful manuscript to a publisher. It is better that you discover a major organizational problem with your project than the publisher does, right?

Once you have separated your book into logical chapters, title them and write a 200-800 (or so) word description of each.

ADDITIONS
Be sure to list, in your Chapter Outline, your resource list (if applicable) bibliography and index, for example.

RESOURCE LIST
Nonfiction books are more useful when they include a resource list where readers can go to locate additional information. This might include books, Web sites and listings of appropriate organizations. You do not need to include the entire Resource List in your book proposal. Just outline the types of resources you plan to include or, perhaps, the number of resources you will list.

BIBLIOGRAPHY
A bibliography is a list of books and other materials that you used when researching your book. These are particularly useful for historical books. You may want to include one in your book. If so, mention this in your Book Proposal.

INDEX
While all books need a Table of Contents (the list of chapter titles at the front of the book), most nonfiction books should also have an index. There are programs now that you can use to create your index.

I am still inclined to prepare my indexes by hand. An index is vital to some books and highly convenient and recommended for many others.

To create an index, go through your completed manuscript once it has the final page numbers. Select key words and locate these words within the text. I find it helpful in preparing my indexes, to locate an index that I consider complete and useful and I design mine similarly. State in your book proposal if you plan to include an index.

ENHANCEMENTS
I'd also like to mention an optional portion that I use in some of my book proposals. And you may consider including this feature in yours. I call this the Enhancements Page. This is where I list the experts I'll be working with on this project and their affiliations. I might also mention here, the illustrations or photos I have in mind for this manuscript. For my Fathering and Fatherhood book (yet, unpublished), I explained on the Enhancements Page that I envisioned starting each chapter with a photo of a dad with his child. I also listed over thirty agencies that I had contacted related to this project. If you're working with an illustrator, mention that here and include samples of the illustrations (never send originals). Perhaps, you will quote famous people at the beginning of each chapter. Share this information with the publisher through the Enhancements Page.

Yes, you will mention some of the experts you plan to quote earlier in the book proposal—in the Synopsis, for example and perhaps also in some of the chapter descriptions. But, when you have done a tremendous amount of research and you've contacted a large number of experts and other sources, it becomes cumbersome to list them all in these sections. You want your Synopsis and Chapter Outline to flow. That's why I include this impressive information on a separate page and title it, Enhancements.

Will you have an expert write the foreword for your book or provide a testimonial for the back cover? Mention this on the Enhancements Page, too. If it is someone of note, you will also want to include this news in your cover letter.

ASSIGNMENT
Your assignment today is to start your Chapter Outline.

Those of you who have been working on each segment of your proposal in sequence are getting closer and closer to having a finished book proposal. Once your Chapter Outline is complete, you will need to write a few sample chapters and you will be ready to go.

You'll be surprised at how quickly and easily your chapters will come together once you have determined your chapter breaks. This is another beauty of the book proposal—it actually serves to help you write the book. When you are ready, you simply expand on the material in the Chapter Outline.

SAMPLE CHAPTER OUTLINE
Here is a portion of the chapter outline for one of my book proposals. Note: While I had a publisher interested in this book (*Alone But Not Lonely, Keys to Happy, Healthy Solitary Living*) and we worked together on it for several months, I ended up deciding against going with this publisher. I received an acceptance letter for another manuscript about this time and didn't move forward with this one

Alone But Not Lonely
Chapter 1: Understanding Your Loneliness

If you live by yourself, you're not alone. One-quarter of American households are operated single-handedly, and these numbers are on the rise. We're living longer. An individual who outlives a spouse, for example, might carry on alone for twenty years or more. We're divorcing more often and staying single longer. The divorce rate is over fifty percent now and a whopping forty-one percent of adults today never marry at all. Something else that contributes to solitary living in America is our tendency to disconnect from extended family support.

Yes, we're an increasingly independent society, but we're also becoming more lonely. This chapter will explore what loneliness is, how feelings of loneliness are triggered and how it affects us. I'll examine two basic kinds of loneliness: situational loneliness (caused by the loss of a loved one, divorce,

54

empty nest syndrome or a move to a new community, for example) and emotional loneliness (based in shyness and feelings of being unloved and unlovable).

For many, *singlehood* is a state of non-being. Why do we see our lives as temporary and ourselves as *less than* when we're not in a relationship? Why do we need the approval of others in order to feel validated? Why does it seem that we're wasting time unless someone is sharing in a task or an activity with us? Why does time alone often make us uneasy?

Part of the answer lies in our childhood. In this chapter, we'll explore the impact childhood conditioning has on our concept of being alone. Think about it, being alone as a child usually meant forced isolation or rejection. You were sent to your room to be alone as punishment for bad behavior. Perhaps you recall being left out of activities as a child—maybe you were excluded by your peers or your parents didn't allow you to go somewhere you wanted to go. Do you remember how you felt? Isolated? Abandoned? Rejected?

If your parents were like most, they had a part in your grown-up feelings about being alone. Did your parents express concern for your safety whenever you stayed home alone as a child? Did they lecture you about the dangers of walking home alone from school or the movies?

And what about the movies you saw? Those that frightened you most usually featured someone who was home alone.

Like it or not, there *is* a stigma attached to the concept of living alone. Even those men and women who have chosen to be alone either temporarily or as a way of life, are sometimes ashamed to reveal this to others for fear they'll be thought of as somehow defective.
Being alone does not in and of itself create loneliness. Loneliness is not an involuntary sensation like a leg cramp. Like anger, resentment, joy and love, it's triggered by our own thoughts and personal belief system.

There's no doubt that living alone takes some adjustment. Just as it's necessary to learn how to live together with a new spouse or a child in the home, you must learn how to live alone.

We've all read the results of studies wherein experts have determined that living alone is bad for one's health. "Married people are healthier and live longer than single people," experts dared to report. A second look at those studies, however, reveal that there are no differences in the overall health and mortality rate between happily married and happily single individuals. Unhappily married people tested as poorly as unhappy singles. And, in this study, the majority of singles (particularly those who were recently divorced) were not coping well with being alone. We know now that it's not the state of being alone that creates illness, it's the way you handle that state.

Because events that trigger feelings of loneliness can enter anyone's life at any time, it's wise to be prepared. Learn to live life to the fullest whether your home is bursting at the seams with family or you live alone.

Through information, anecdotes and exercises, this chapter will introduce the concept that, although the state of being alone may not be of your making or even of your liking, loneliness is a choice. It's not the fact of being alone that's the problem, it's your way of handling it that causes either misery or joy.

Two major things will happen as a result of reading this book: you'll never have to suffer the pain of loneliness again and you'll discover the joy in solitude.

Chapter 2: Finding and Facing Your Loneliness Issues

This chapter will bring the reader face-to-face with their particular loneliness issues through an exploration of more than half dozen real life scenarios. Included will be the inspiring story of a young mother whose husband often traveled on business and who was miserable in his absence until she changed her mind and changed her life. This chapter will also feature stories of two widows—one still wallowing in her sadness five years later and the other seemingly sailing through life with ease. We'll find out why. We'll view the lives of a couple of divorcees and explore their greatest difficulties and their remedies. We'll also examine the problems one couple had reconnecting socially after relocating and how they overcame them.

The specific loneliness issues outlined through these scenarios will include fear and fear-based problems, anger, feelings of abandonment and rejection, boredom, low self-esteem, lack of motivation and creativity in living single whether due to loss and grief or lack of imagination, dependency—feeling like a non-person in a coupled world and poor life-management skills. Subsequent chapters will, of course, address and explore each of these loneliness issues and coach the reader in resolving them.

Chapter 3: Loneliness and Self-Abuse
Often individuals alone aren't as caring toward themselves as they are when they're caring for someone else. We typically prepare more well-balanced and palatable meals when there's someone dining with us. We keep our space and ourselves more tidy as a courtesy to others. And we generally maintain more reasonable habits and schedules when there's someone else in the house.

When alone, however, you're more apt to forget your good-for-you routine and this is a form of self-abuse. Instead of eating the salad you know you should have at your regular dinner hour and getting to bed early on a work night, when alone, you're tendency might be to sit amidst clutter wearing faded sweats while staying up late eating potato chips and drinking chocolate milk out of the carton. Granted, this minor form of self-abuse is probably nothing more than a blatant act of rebellion. Being alone, after all, provides the opportunity to rebel against every authority figure who has ever ticked you off.

Beware of self-abuse when you're alone, however, as it can easily get out of hand. The chronically lonely, and those who harbor fear of being alone, often become involved in extremely destructive behavior by virtue of the fact of their aloneness—behaviors such as: alcohol and drug abuse, promiscuity, workaholism, social deprivation, social obsessions, over-eating and over-spending.

This chapter will help the reader evaluate their particular behavior pattern and honestly determine if they're on a destructive path.

Book Proposal Class

8

PUTTING IT ALL TOGETHER

We have had seven sessions together working on your proposal. This seems like a long time and a lot of work. If you had devoted eight-hour workdays to this project, you should have a well-written, well-organized book proposal by now. I timed myself the last time I wrote a book proposal and it took me exactly a week to complete the proposal and two sample chapters.

I had a private communication with one student during the seventh week of one Book Proposal Course. I believe that every student could benefit from what I told her. Here it is:

"Your chapter outline should reflect your writing skills while entertaining and informing the publisher. You want him to see your book as something that will engage thousands of consumers. If he doesn't see dollar signs while he is studying your book proposal, he probably won't be interested. And thousands of eager consumers compute into dollars for him (and you)."

I would strongly urge you to make your proposal a priority as soon as possible and complete it while these lectures and your research are fresh in your mind. It isn't even necessary to have those eight hours each day to work on it. If you could even spare two hours each day to focus on this project, you'll be surprised at how quickly it will come together.

I can't tell you how many people I meet both online and off who express a fervent desire to write a book or to find a publisher for their book, but who can't find the time or the motivation to do the necessary work. Where there's a will there's a way and sometimes it takes personal sacrifice.

MY STORY
I became despondent at one point in my life because I had to get a job. I thought I would have to work full-time from now on and would never be able to write again. I had to find a way to write or I would surely shrivel up and die. So I started getting up at 4 a.m. each morning and I would write for two hours before taking my walk and getting ready for work. I completed an entire book in eight-months time on this schedule. Encouraged beyond belief, I started using those two hours each morning to build my article-writing business and within a year, I was able to quit the job and become a full-time writer. I've been writing for publication since 1973 and writing has been my fulltime work—how I earn my living—since 1989.

ORGANIZING AND SENDING YOUR BOOK PROPOSAL
As for assembling the proposal: I send mine loose—not in a binder. While some publishers appreciate receiving manuscripts and book proposals in binders, others do not. Unless the Submission Guidelines ask for the proposal to be bound, I would send it loose.

There are differences of opinion as to how the proposal should be organized. Jeff Herman and Debra Adams, authors of *Write the Perfect Book Proposal* and I agree on this order:

Cover Letter
Title Page
Synopsis or Overview
Marketing Section—Promotional Pages
Market Analysis—Competitive Works
About the Author
Chapter Outline
Sample Chapters

I recommend numbering the pages to make it easier for the publisher to keep the proposal in order. I sometimes number the proposal pages using Roman Numerals and I use regular numbers for my sample chapters.

Use appropriate headings for the Synopsis, Promotions Pages, Market Analysis, About the Author and Chapter Outline, for example. The Cover Letter and Title Page are self-explanatory.

Make sure that your contact information is prominently displayed. Your name, address, phone number, fax number and email address should appear on your cover letter, at least. It wouldn't hurt to repeat it maybe on your About the Author page and again at the top of the first page of your first chapter. It is always a good idea to print your book title and maybe your last name at the top right of each page of your proposal.

Never send your only original copy. This may seem elementary, but just recently, I received a very large manuscript from an author who claimed it was his only copy. This was a risky move on his part, especially since he sent it without notifying me. Of course, it got lost and that was because he had my address wrong. And would you believe, he had no return address on the package? Unbelievable! I did locate the package (thanks to the fact that I live in a small town) and I shipped it back to him the next day.

Always enclose a self-addressed-stamped envelope for a return reply. If you want the proposal returned, enclose packaging with proper postage. If you don't care about having the proposal returned, simply enclose a size 10 (letter-size) envelope, of course addressed and stamped.

Not all publishers respect and honor your sense of professionalism and attention to detail. Some of them do not respond to a query letter no matter how easy you make it for them to. Some will toss out an unwanted manuscript and your post-paid mailer. Generally, however, when a package has been requested, it is handled appropriately.

SIMULTANEOUS SUBMISSIONS

Send your query letter to more than one publisher at a time. This saves time and wear and tear on your nerves. Some publishers are okay with simultaneous book proposal submissions. But you rarely send a manuscript to more than one publisher at a time. If you do, make sure that it is okay with both parties.

PUBLISHER FOLLOW-UP

Most publishers note on their Submission Guidelines, when you can expect their response to a query letter, book proposal and manuscript submission. Typically, they promise to respond to a query letter in anywhere from one to three months and a book proposal or manuscript from one to eight months. While most publishers honor their word, some are lax in responding and others never respond. What is an author to do? When is it appropriate to follow-up on a submission?

Here's my rule of thumb:

Query Letter—send a tracer letter (follow-up letter of inquiry) one to two weeks after the publisher's projected response time. If their Guidelines state that they will generally respond in four weeks, a tracer is appropriate after five or six weeks. An email tracer letter is often more effective and convenient. Some publishers do not respond to email from authors, however.

Book Proposal—send a letter of inquiry (Did you receive my package?) after about three weeks. Sometimes the mails fail and you must resubmit. Most often, however, the package is eventually found at the publishing house in a stack on somebody else's desk. A missing package can be a blessing. I find that publishers/editors pay extra attention to a package that lost its way and is being reshipped. Of course, it is appropriate to call, email or write after making the second submission attempt.

Once you know that the package has been received, wait until at least two weeks past the publisher's projected response time to inquire as to the status of your proposal.

Manuscript—follow the suggestion (above) for a book proposal. Keep any anxiety you might feel out of the correspondence. Remain calm and professional. It is easy to lose patience with a lackadaisical publisher. Some of them seem to be busy, disorganized people—with little regard for the author. Do you really want to work with this kind of person? On the other hand, you don't want to lose your chance to be published. I advise jumping through the hoops for as long as there are hoops available, while asserting your need for acknowledgement and information. But I advise against signing with a publisher who seems difficult to work with.

I fired a publisher this year. He accepted my book, *The Right Way to Write, Publish and Sell Your Book*—one that I am quite eager to have published. He said that an advance and a contract would be forthcoming. I went right to work writing the book while trying to nudge this publisher into some sort of action. All I got from him for the next three months was an occasional brief email saying how busy he was and that the contract was coming.

It's still hard for me to believe what happened next. I finally received a contract by fax—one that had been used for another author. The name and terms were whited out. The publisher said that they lost the original contract and he asked me if I would retype it. Once he had a fresh contract, he would send me a copy to sign. He said there was $50 in it for me. Okay, so I retyped the very simple contract and attached it to an email for him. Another month went by. The day that I finished the book, I sent this publisher an email saying that I would not be interested in trying to work with him—that I'd be seeking publication elsewhere. I included an invoice for the $50 he still owed me.

Never forget that you have options, even in the competitive world of publishing. I'm actually considering self-publishing this book. With the contacts and prominence I have in the publishing/writing field, I can probably do as well promoting it as most publishers. And I rather like the idea of receiving the full profit instead of a measly twelve or fifteen percent ($2 to $3 per book).

ADDITIONAL RESOURCES

I'd like to suggest that each of you visit my Web site: http://www.matilijapress.com. Check out my books. I'm positive that I have books that would be of value to you. Two of them come to mind. *The Successful Writer's Handbook* is a really fantastic 180-page book filled with all sorts of help for freelance writers and authors. This book covers:

- Steps to preparing a book proposal and a query letter.
- How to establish yourself as a writer.
- How to find writing work that fulfills your passion.
- How to avoid the pitfalls of writing as a business.
- Seven rules for crushing writers block.

If you want to produce articles for money or in order to promote your book (my favorite book promotion activity), I cover:

- Seven steps to getting your articles published.
- How to come up with article ideas.
- The anatomy of an article.
- How to recycle your articles.

I have a section on writing for niche markets, I talk about working with a publisher, self-publishing and I include a huge section on book promotion (something that all of you will need to know about).

Do you want to know how to:

- speak well in public?
- take care of the writer within?
- write a successful query letter?
- network successfully with other writers

And the resources for writers section in this book is phenomenal.

You will also want to check out my book, *Over 75 Good Ideas for Promoting Your Book*. Some publishers suggest that their authors purchase this book before they will work with that author. This is a book full of no and low-cost promotional ideas. The ideas in this book may even help you to complete your promotions portion of your book proposal.

Hopefully, you'll soon find my latest book, *The Right Way to Write, Publish and Sell Your Book* or *A Guide to Successful Authorship.* This is the ultimate book for any hopeful first-time or anytime author as it covers everything from POD publishing to finding a publisher and agent to self-publishing and promotion. This could become one of the industry's most definitive authoring guides. I know it will save a lot of hopeful authors from making some of the most common, expensive and devastating mistakes with their first book projects.

I invite you to visit the SPAWN Web site at http://www.spawn.org. You will be amazed at the volume of valuable information on the Web site and this is just the tip of the iceberg. Be sure to subscribe to the free newsletter. Become a member and you'll have access to the extremely newsy *SPAWN Market Update*

I look forward to receiving your book proposal/publishing success stories. Plfry620@yahoo.com. And be sure to let me know if you have any questions I can help you with.

Index

About the Author, 44-49; sample, 45-46, 46-49
Adams, Deborah, 11, 59
Agents, how to find one, 17
Author's Guidelines (See Submission Guidelines)
Bibliography, 52
Book Proposal, why write one, 1, 3-5; what publishers want, 2-3;
    nonfiction,3; novel, 3; your business plan, 3-4; organizing, 58-61;
    sending, 59; tracer letter for, 61
Book Signing, 30; tips for authors, 31-33
Bookstore sales, 26, 27-28
Chapter Outline, 50-57; examples, 50-52; sample, 54-57
Comparison of Competitive Works (See Market Analysis)
Competition (See Market Analysis)
Cover letter, 6-7; sample, 13-14
Enhancements, 53
Guidelines for Authors (See Submission Guidelines)
Herman, Jeff, 11, 16, 59
Index, writing one, 52-53
ISBN, 5, 35
Literary Market Place, 2, 10, 17
Mailing List, 30
Market Analysis, 39-49; sample, 41-42
One-sentence challenge, 16-17, 23
Organize your book, 22
Organize your book proposal, 58-64
Over 75 Good Ideas for Promoting Your Book, 16, 37, 48, 63
Overview (See Synopsis)
POD Publishers, 5-6
Poynter, Dan, 18, 37
Premium Item, 29-30
Promote Your Book Before it's a Book, 35-36
Promotion, author must promote, 17; promotions section, 25-43;
    examples from my book proposals, 28-29;
    sample marketing section, 37-38
Publisher, approaching, 1-2, 11; POD, 5-6; locating, 10-11, 17-18;
    number of, 18; what he wants, 58; lack of professionalism, 60;
    follow up, 61, 62
Query Letter, 1, 6; sample, 11-13; send tracer, 61
Resources, 63-64
Resource List, 52
Right Way to Write, Publish and Sell Your Book, 12, 46, 62, 64

SASE (Self-Addressed-Stamped Envelope), 2, 3, 60
Self-publishing, 4, 5, 8, 10, 12, 18, 27, 35, 40, 62, 64
Simultaneous Submissions, 61
SPAWN (Small Publishers, Artists and Writers Network), 27, 31, 46, 47, 64
Specialty Stores, 28
Submission Guidelines, 1, 2-3, 7, 10, 59, 61
Successful Writer's Handbook, 11, 38, 48, 63
Synopsis, 15-24; tips for writing, 22-24; example, 18-21
Table of Contents, 10
Target Audience, 25-27
Title, choosing, 8-10
Title Page, 7
Tracer Letters, 61
Word Count, 7-8
Writing a book, how long does it take, 6-7
Writer's Market, 2, 10, 17, 18, 28
Writing Tips, 22-23